101
USES
FOR A

MAINE
COON
CAT

Down East Books

Published by Down East Books
An imprint of Globe Pequot
Trade Division of The Rowman & Littlefield Publishing Group, Inc.
4501 Forbes Boulevard, Suite 200, Lanham, Maryland 20706
www.rowman.com

Unit A, Whitacre Mews, 26-34 Stannary Street, London SE11 4AB, United Kingdom

Distributed by NATIONAL BOOK NETWORK

Design by Lynda Chilton, Chilton Creative

Photographs: Lynn Karlin, cover, pgs.6, 128; Grey Geezer, p.126; Takashi Hoshoshima, p.120; Sage Ross, p.116; Hillary Steinau, p.108; Liza Gardner Walsh, p.26; Dreamstime, pgs. 4-9, 12-18, 20, 26-29, 32-34, 39-43, 46-47, 51-56, 60, 64, 68-72, 78-79, 82, 89-90, 92-93, 96-97, 102, 103, 105-107, 110-113, 121, 127; Shutterstock, pgs. 3, 11, 30, 35, 37, 44-45, 50, 58-59, 61, 66, 75, 77, 83, 87, 90, 94, 99, 100, 101, 109, 116-117, 122-123, 132-133; 136; Thinkstock, pgs. 22-23, 36, 48-49, 62-63, 65, 67, 73, 85, 91, 95, 129.

British Library Cataloguing in Publication Information Available

Library of Congress Cataloging-in-Publication Data Available

ISBN 978-1-60893-605-2 (cloth : alk. paper)
ISBN 978-1-60893-606-9 (electronic)

♾™ The paper used in this publication meets the minimum requirements of American National Standard for Information Sciences—Permanence of Paper for Printed Library Materials, ANSI/NISO Z39.48-1992.

Printed in the United States of America

LOOKOUT

ABOMINABLE
SNOW CAT

BOOT
WARMER

Drill
Sargeant

GARDENER

Piano
Tuner

LIBRARIAN

CARPET
SWEEPER

A GOOD
LISTENER...

...WHO WON'T BETRAY YOUR SECRETS

ARBORIST

Tightrope WALKER

TAPE
MEASURE

FLORIST

TRIBBLE

BOOKMARK

BASKET CASE

DOG
SITTER

Camouflage

Stocking Stuffers

POLAR EXPLORER

HIDE & SEEK
PARTNER

NERVOUS
NELLY

Shipping
CLERK

PLUMBER

MONA LISA

Santa's Helper

POSSE

Sleeping
BEAUTY

Constant
Companion

TOWEL BOY

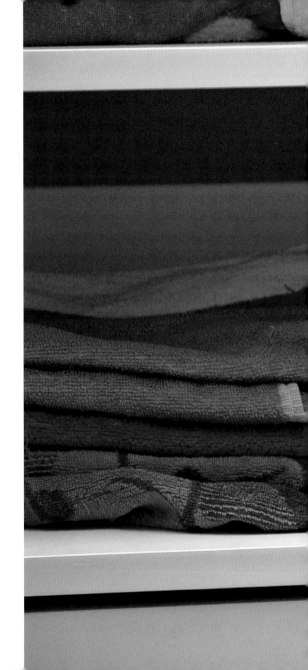

TOUGH
NEGOTIATOR

LEAF
PEEPER

Sassmaster

STAND-UP COMIC

Supercat

59

ROCK HOUND

BED
WARMER

BIRD-WATCHER

DISHWASHER

65⫰

RACE CAR
DRIVER

CO-CONSPIRATOR

67

BUTCH AND SUNDANCE

DAYDREAMER

HECKLER

DeNiro
STAND-IN

ELF
ON A
SHELF

75§

YOGA
INSTRUCTOR

SPHINX

FERN

GENTLE
GIANT

GARGOYLE

83♂

SUNBATHER

HOT
DATE

LOG
JAM

87

PACIFIST

Nature
Guide

FARMER

BIRDBATH

CLOSE TALKER

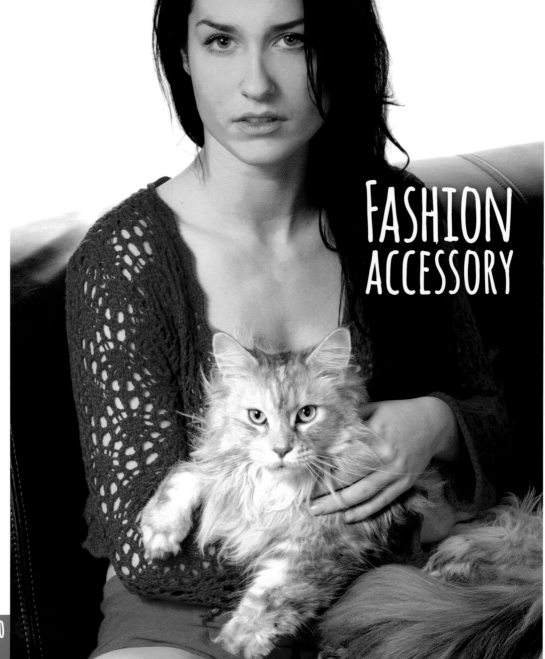

FASHION
ACCESSORY

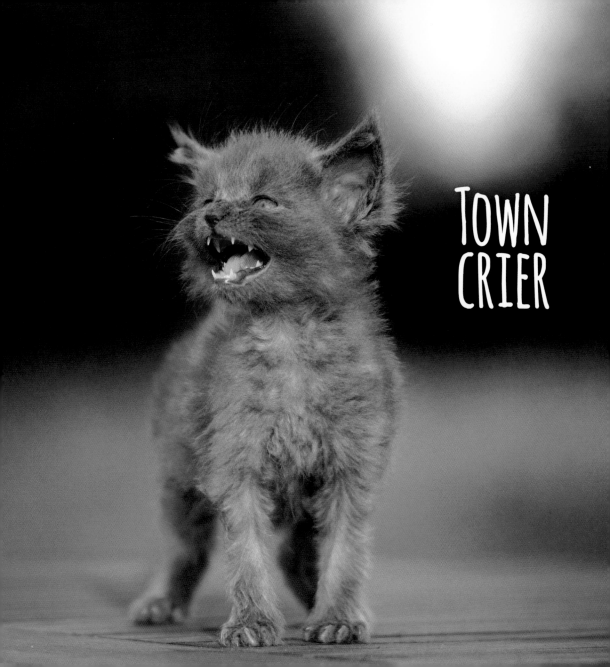

TOWN CRIER

LUMBERJACK

GREAT WHITE HUNTER

FURNITURE TESTER

CHEERLEADER

Forest Fire
Lookout

CONTORTIONIST

Deep Thinker

NOBILITY

ROAD
CONSTRUCTION
WORKER

Orator

ORCHARD
KEEPER

THE JOKER

PRIZEFIGHTER

PEEK-A-BOO

DUSTMOP

SHOCK
AND AWE

HIGH DIVER

STARGAZER

Sourpuss

GUINEA PIG

TUMBLEWEED

HERBALIST

ARCHITECT

Owl

BOTANIST

DETECTIVE

SHREDDER

THE
BEE
GEES

PHYSICIAN'S ASSISTANT